Table of Contents

Statement of National Policy

The goal of this National Action Plan on Women, Peace, and Security is as simple as it is profound: to empower half the world's population as equal partners in preventing conflict and building peace in countries threatened and affected by war, violence, and insecurity. Achieving this goal is critical to our national and global security.

Deadly conflicts can be more effectively avoided, and peace can be best forged and sustained, when women become equal partners in all aspects of peace-building and conflict prevention, when their lives are protected, their experiences considered, and their voices heard.

As directed by the Executive Order signed by President Obama entitled Instituting a National Action Plan on Women, Peace, and Security, this Plan describes the course the United States Government will take to accelerate, institutionalize, and better coordinate our efforts to advance women's inclusion in peace negotiations, peacebuilding activities, and conflict prevention; to protect women from sexual and gender-based violence; and to ensure equal access to relief and recovery assistance, in areas of conflict and insecurity. It is guided by the following five principles:

First, the engagement and protection of women as agents of peace and stability will be **central** to the United States' efforts to promote security, prevent, respond to, and resolve conflict, and rebuild societies.

Second, by building on the goals for gender integration described in the United States National Security Strategy and the Quadrennial Diplomacy and Development Review, the United States' efforts on Women, Peace, and Security will **complement** and enhance existing initiatives to advance gender equality and women's empowerment, ensure respect for human rights, and address the needs of vulnerable populations in crisis and conflict environments.

> The U.S. National Action Plan on Women, Peace, and Security builds upon the goals for gender integration described in the U.S. National Security Strategy and the 2010 Quadrennial Diplomacy and Development Review. Gender integration involves identifying and addressing, in all our policies and programs, gender differences and inequalities, as well as the roles of women and men. The goal of gender integration or "mainstreaming" is to promote gender equality and improve programming and policy outcomes.

Third, in executing this policy, the United States will be guided by the principle of **inclusion**, seeking out the views and participation of a wide variety of stakeholders—women and girls, men and boys, and members of marginalized groups, including youth, ethnic, racial or religious minorities, persons with disabilities, displaced persons and indigenous peoples, lesbian, gay, bisexual and transgender (LGBT) individuals, and people from all socioeconomic strata.

Fourth, in order to maximize the impact of this Plan, the United States will ensure that activities in support of Women, Peace and Security are **coordinated** among all relevant departments and agencies

(agencies) of the government, integrated into relevant United States foreign policy initiatives, and enhanced by engagement with international partners.

Finally, United States Government agencies will be **accountable** for the implementation of the policies and initiatives endorsed in this Plan.

Above all, this National Action Plan expresses the United States' unqualified commitment to integrating women's views and perspectives fully into our diplomatic, security, and development efforts—not simply as beneficiaries, but as agents of peace, reconciliation, development, growth, and stability. We welcome this opportunity to work with our international partners to make the promise of this commitment real, to advance implementation of United Nations (UN) Security Council Resolution 1325, and to make significant progress toward the goal of sustainable peace and security for all.

The Case for Women in Peace and Security

Women as Equal Participants in Conflict Resolution

More than half of all peace agreements fail within the first 10 years of signature. In many countries, high levels of violence continue to afflict communities long after wars have officially ceased. Peace accords are too often negotiated only between the small number of armed combatants who originally fought the war—groups whose experiences on the battlefield are not easily transferred to the difficult task of building peace.

First Lady Michelle Obama and Secretary of State Hillary Clinton pose with awardees at the 2011 International Women of Courage award ceremony at the State Department.
Photo Credit: State Department

When included as meaningful participants, women enlarge the scope of agreements to include the broader set of critical societal priorities and needs required for lasting and just peace. In Northern Ireland, for example, women negotiators secured commitments in the 1998 Good Friday Agreement to involve young people and victims of violence in reconciliation; to accelerate the release and reintegration of political prisoners; and to ensure an integrated education system and integrated housing. In the 1990s, Guatemalan women involved in negotiations to end a 36-year civil war secured important protections for labor and indigenous rights as well as guarantees of a balance in civilian and military power. They also enshrined commitments to women's equal rights and participation in the peace accords. In post-apartheid South Africa, more than 70 organizations united under the Women's National Coalition to outline fundamental rights for women in the "Women's Charter for Effective Equality." The charter directly resulted in a constitution that not only protects women's equal rights, but also contains many important rights that apply to all members of society: the right to education, the freedoms of religion and expression, and the right to security of person. In 2003, Liberian women acting largely outside of formal negotiations brought their demands into the streets and reinforced mediators' efforts to secure a peace that would end that country's devastating civil war.

Even when peace processes have failed to end conflict conclusively, women have positively influenced efforts to advance security and stability via negotiations. In 2006, Ugandan women involved in peace talks between the Ugandan government and representatives of the Lord's Resistance Army secured a compensation fund for victims of violence, including gender-based violence, and ensured that health and education for former combatants were addressed explicitly in negotiated protocols; although the accord was never implemented, women's priorities have been reflected in Northern Ugandan recovery efforts and women have continued to push for transparency in reconstruction. Darfurian women, who provided gender expertise to African Union-mediated talks in 2005, shined a spotlight on the need to provide protection for the vulnerable and displaced and highlighted a wide range of critical gender concerns related to land rights and physical security. These women inserted critical issues into the talks that negotiators had previously ignored.

Institutionalizing Our Commitment to Women as Agents of Positive Change

As noted in the U.S. National Security Strategy, "Experience shows that countries are more peaceful and prosperous when women are accorded full and equal rights and opportunity." In order to bring about the peace and prosperity we seek, the United States is promoting better understanding and integration of gender issues across all our agencies.

The Department of State and U.S. Agency for International Development (USAID) are implementing reforms initiated through the 2010 Quadrennial Diplomacy and Development Review (QDDR) related to support for women and girls abroad in the realms of policy development, budget planning, and personnel training. The new positions of the Department of State's Ambassador-at-Large for Global Women's Issues and USAID's Senior Coordinator for Gender Equality and Women's Empowerment ensure that women's rights and concerns remain at the core of U.S. foreign policy. USAID's policy framework highlights a commitment to gender equality and female empowerment as a key operational principle, while USAID's revised Policy on Gender Equality and Female Empowerment will institutionalize our commitment throughout U.S. development and humanitarian assistance activities. In all countries, including those affected by crisis and conflict, USAID mandates that development and humanitarian assistance activities be informed by gender analysis. Expanded guidance on gender integration in Country Development Cooperation Strategies, Programming, Project Design, and Learning and Evaluation tools are helping ensure programs reduce gender disparities and promote equal access for women and men to political, economic, and social resources and opportunities. In order to address forced labor and sexual exploitation, USAID is also revising its Counter Trafficking in Persons (C-TIP) Policy, which will include a specific objective aimed at increasing USAID investments in TIP prevention and protection in conflict and crisis-affected areas. Finally, foreign assistance indicators tracking the performance of programs implemented by USAID and the Department of State now include specific indicators on gender equality, women's empowerment, sexual and gender-based violence (SGBV) prevention and response, and women's participation in peacebuilding.

The Department of Defense (DOD) has dedicated staff responsible for addressing gender considerations in keeping with DOD's mission. Within the Office of the Secretary of Defense, the Office of the Undersecretary of Defense for Policy coordinates the development and implementation of DOD's efforts on Women, Peace, and Security. The Office of the Undersecretary of Defense for Personnel and Readiness coordinates the Department's efforts on sexual assault prevention and response, and combating trafficking in persons. For the Military Services, the Defense Advisory Committee on Women in the Services advises on policies related to the recruitment, retention, treatment, and integration of women into U.S. Armed Forces. Around the world, several of DOD's Combatant Commands have made gender issues a focus. U.S. Africa Command has established a Gender Working Group focused on integrating gender considerations across the command's programs and engagements with African militaries. In Afghanistan, U.S. Central Command and NATO's International Security Assistance Force (ISAF) have established gender advisors to assist commanders in identifying the differing effects a potential operation may have on local men and women. In addition, the Marine Corps' Female Engagement Teams and the Army's Cultural Support Teams are providing new avenues for women Marines and soldiers to support ongoing operations and engage women in local populations.

Despite this positive record, since 1992 women have represented fewer than three percent of mediators and eight percent of negotiators to major peace processes, numbers that have not markedly improved since the passage over a decade ago of the landmark UN Security Council Resolution 1325. While the number of women heading UN field missions has increased, the UN has never appointed a woman as a lead mediator. In country after country, women who risked their lives to confront and persuade armed actors to join peace negotiations and foster the trust necessary to initiate negotiations have found themselves sidelined once official talks began. This exclusion is as much a blow to peace and international security efforts as it is to women.

U.S. Marines with Marine Expeditionary Brigade-Afghanistan and members of a Female Engagement Team (FET) use an interpreter to interact with Afghan women and children in Helmand province, Afghanistan. *Photo Credit: Sgt. Evan Barragan/U.S. Marine Corps*

The voices and concerns of women who endured violence and supported communities during conflict, and who will carry much of the burden of healing and rebuilding communities in peacetime, are routinely absent from or overlooked at the negotiating table. This exclusion often carries over into related post-conflict efforts to rebuild, to strengthen peace by reforming the security sector, and to redress past grievances and abuses. Peace agreements that focus solely on ending the fighting fail to address the vital tasks necessary for sustaining a genuine peace: providing security and basic services, building trust amongst opposing parties, fostering institutions that can uphold the rule of law, and promoting legitimately-elected leadership. Engaging women as leaders and participants can help close this gap and offer a chance for more lasting peace agreements.

Evidence from around the world and across cultures shows that integrating women and gender considerations into peace-building processes helps promote democratic governance and long-term stability. In order to achieve these goals, women need to be able to play a role in building and participating in the full range of decision-making institutions in their countries. These institutions, from civil society to the judicial and security sectors, must also be responsive to and informed by women's demands.

Promoting Women's Participation in Peacebuilding: Afghanistan

Since 2001, the United States has worked with the women of Afghanistan to ensure that they take part in all key country-wide political decision-making processes. Afghan women have advocated successfully for protections for women's rights in the 2004 Constitution, including a 25 percent quota for female representation in Parliament. More than 400 candidates for the 2011 parliamentary elections were women, representing a sizeable increase since the 2005 parliamentary elections. Today, women hold 69 of the 249 seats in the Afghan National Assembly (68 of which are constitutionally mandated). Three women serve as Cabinet members, and many others participate in provincial assemblies.

In order to secure Afghanistan's long-term stability and development, we will continue to work with the international community and Afghan civil society to help ensure women participate at all levels of decision-making and governance. Afghan women are involved in the Afghan Peace and Reintegration Program, and a gender advisor now works on the Joint Secretariat charged with implementing the program. Nine out of the 68 members of the policy-making High Peace Council are women, and women are beginning to serve on Provincial-level Peace and Reintegration Councils. The United States is insisting that reconciled Taliban agree to abide by the Afghan Constitution, including its provisions on the rights of women and minorities. There is no question that the women of Afghanistan still must travel a long road before they achieve full equality. We are committed to supporting their entire journey.

Protections for Women During and After Conflict

Even as we work to include more women in peace negotiations, we must make stronger and more comprehensive efforts to protect them from violence both during and after conflict. Two decades into the 21st century, conflict remains primarily an intra-state phenomenon. Civilians bear the overwhelming brunt of today's wars. Starvation and disease prey primarily upon women, children, and the elderly.

Amidst such suffering, in many conflict zones around the world women and girls are deliberately targeted and attacked, often with impunity. Forced displacement associated with crisis and conflict exposes refugees and internally displaced persons, particularly women and girls, to additional risks of violence and exploitation. Violence against women, particularly forms of sexual violence including rape, sexual assault, mutilation, forced prostitution, and sexual slavery, is increasingly recognized as a facet of many recent conflicts, from the Balkans to Africa.

Sexual and gender-based violence (SGBV) in conflict and situations of extreme violence is at times deployed as a deliberate tactic for purposes of humiliation, terror, societal destruction, and ethnic cleansing. In other circumstances sexual violence is opportunistic.

In places where wars have officially come to an end, women and girls often continue to be plagued by high levels of violence and insecurity; widespread impunity and breakdowns in the rule of law can contribute to high rates of gender-based and domestic violence. Thus, increased violence against women can be a cause and a consequence of a societal breakdown. When countries are not experiencing active conflict, evidence shows that violence against women can be a primary indicator of a nation's stability, security, and propensity toward internal or external conflict. This indicator may be as telling as levels of democracy or wealth.

Protecting Women from Sexual and Gender-Based Violence (SGBV)

The United States has prioritized efforts to prevent and respond to sexual and gender-based violence (SGBV), including sexual exploitation and abuse (SEA), in conflict situations around the world. Since 2010, USAID has programmed over $17.5 million in humanitarian assistance funds to prevent and respond to SGBV in disasters and conflicts, reaching nearly 3 million beneficiaries in 12 countries. Over the same timeframe, the State Department has programmed more than $21.5 million in humanitarian assistance funds to prevent and respond to SGBV in displacement crises. The Department of Justice, through its human trafficking and justice-sector development programs, has actively promoted efforts to increase the commitment and capacity of partner countries to investigate, prosecute, and deter gender-based exploitation. The Department of Homeland Security counters human trafficking, exploitation, and violence against women by administering humanitarian immigration benefits, collaborating with law enforcement abroad, and promoting international partnerships and public awareness. In recent years the U.S. Centers for Disease Control and Prevention (CDC) have brought public health and epidemiologic principles to the aid of women and girls affected by complex humanitarian emergencies in Liberia, Sri Lanka, Haiti and Uganda by documenting the magnitude and risks of SGBV and using data to improve programs and inform policy-making. In collaboration with the Office of the UN High Commissioner for Refugees, CDC has employed enhanced surveillance systems to monitor SGBV cases in humanitarian situations through the development of the UNHCR health information system, which currently reaches a total of 2.4 million refugees in 18 countries around the world.

In the Democratic Republic of Congo (DRC), the United States has provided legal advice and care and treatment services for well over 100,000 SGBV survivors. These services include mobile clinics that expand the reach of services for survivors of sexual violence, as well as programs that engage men and boys in challenging norms and practices that contribute to rape and domestic violence in their communities. The Unitet States has made efforts to improve accountability by promoting national-level legal reforms, such as the adoption of the 2006 Law Against SGBV and reform of the Family Code, advocacy, and increasing access to legal services to survivors through mobile courts. Instructors from DOD's Defense International Institute of Legal Studies provide training to the Congolese military on preventing SGBV and prosecuting cases through the military court system. In addition, the United States has provided support to the UN Organization Stabilization Mission in the DRC (MONUSCO) for its Prosecution Support Cells, which assist Congolese prosecutors with cases, and its Joint Protection Teams and Joint Human Rights Office to strengthen the protection of victims, witnesses, and judicial officials in cases involving serious abuses of international law.

Despite these critical investments, SGBV remains a terrible reality for communities in conflict affected countries. We are committed to expanding our efforts to identify and build on successful programs, and work with partners to scale up their impact.

No society can restore peace or stability when its population lives in daily fear of rape or other sexual assault—or when the perpetrators of such crimes are not held accountable for their actions. We must take strong, unified action to ensure that victims have access to justice, that those responsible for these crimes are held accountable, and that those who contemplate violence against civilians understand that their actions will carry consequences. Sexual violence in conflict is a security issue that must receive the same level of attention as other threats to individuals in conflict situations. The safety of women and their families must be a top priority for security efforts around the world.

Women and Conflict Prevention Efforts

Measured in lives and livelihoods, stopping cycles of conflict and preventing wars before they occur is the most important way to ensure stability and prosperity around the world. Socio-economic and cultural analyses must inform any effort to forecast and counteract emerging drivers of conflict; examining how risk factors for conflict affect men and women differently improves our understanding of the root causes and consequences of conflict, including vulnerability to mass atrocity. From Kosovo to Rwanda, societies have witnessed rising discrimination and violence against women as early indicators of impending conflict. Tracking and better understanding how these indicators relate to the potential for instability should inform the international community's best practices in preventing conflict before it begins.

Frequently, women have held critical knowledge about impending or escalating conflict, but were overlooked or were unable to report their concerns safely. In Kosovo, women observed the growth of arms caches, but had no one to whom they could report their concerns. Similarly, women in Sierra Leone knew of plans to attack UN peacekeepers, but threats to their personal safety prevented them from relaying that information.

DUE TO COPYRIGHT RESTRICTIONS
SOME OR ALL IMAGES ARE NOT INCLUDED

Kishwar Sultana, director of the Insan Foundation in Pakistan, discusses the importance of including women in peace and security decisions with a cadet from the United States Military Academy at West Point.
Photo credit: Institute for Inclusive Security

With these examples in mind, we will strengthen our efforts to monitor the status of women, and ensure that conflict early warning, atrocity prevention, and conflict mitigation and management endeavors incorporate gender analysis. For example, stateless women and their children face high levels of discrimination and abuse, and their particular risk factors should be assessed. And gender-specific migration patterns or precipitous changes in the status or treatment of women and girls may serve as signals of broader vulnerability to the onset or escalation of conflict or atrocities. This focus will help to ensure that conflict prevention efforts are responsive to sexual and gender-based violence and other forms of violence affecting women and girls, and that our approaches are informed by differences in the experiences of men and women, girls and boys. Further, we will seek to better leverage women's networks and organizations in activities aimed at arresting armed conflict or preventing spirals of violence.

Finally, the United States understands that successful conflict prevention efforts must rest on key investments in women's economic empowerment, education, and health. A growing body of evidence shows that empowering women and reducing gender gaps in health, education, labor markets, and other areas is associated with lower poverty, higher economic growth, greater agricultural productivity, better nutrition and education of children, and other outcomes vital to the success of communities.

Investing in Conflict Prevention through Economic Empowerment, Health, and Education

The United States is committed to amplifying the critical role women can play in conflict prevention and mitigation by participating in early warning systems, leveraging women's networks, and building bridges across divided communities. We also recognize that successful conflict prevention efforts require long-term investments in women's economic empowerment, health, and education. USAID recently launched a new multi-year initiative to support game-changing programs that remove barriers to women owning and managing small and medium-sized enterprises, including legal, social, education and economic barriers, along with rigorous impact evaluation of these efforts.

The United States is also working collaboratively with conflict-affected countries to ensure that women are beneficiaries of priority global development efforts such as the Global Health Initiative and Feed the Future—both for their own well-being and because of the centrality of women to the health and prosperity of families and communities. The Global Health Initiative, for example, aims to reduce maternal mortality by 30 percent in assisted countries, through a range of targeted investments including prenatal care and services, obstetric care, voluntary family planning, HIV testing and counseling, nutritional support, and safe water, sanitation and hygiene interventions. Women are also at the forefront of President Obama's Feed the Future food security initiative, and USAID has recently allocated $5 million for a new Feed the Future program that will promote gender equality and women's empowerment in agriculture and land use.

Education can also mitigate the effects of conflict and provide the basis for long term economic growth and stability. Out of 70 million primary school-aged children not in school, nearly 40 million live in countries affected by armed conflict. It is therefore critical to restore education sites, services and system-wide capacity for children and youth, particularly girls, in conflict-affected or insecure environments. We are working to increase equitable access to education in crisis and conflict environments for 15 million learners, including those with disabilities, by 2015.

Women's Equal Access to the Means for Recovery

Women and children are particularly affected by conflicts, comprising the vast majority of forcibly displaced persons around the world. In many cases, gender roles and norms mean that women are the primary caregivers for families and communities in crisis situations. Women's perspectives are important for ensuring that relief and recovery assistance addresses the needs of the entire affected population. For example, women's participation in camp management committees helps to ensure that displacement camps are safer and assistance programs are more accessible for vulnerable groups such as women, children, and persons with disabilities.

Women and girls also have distinct needs and vulnerabilities that should be addressed within assistance programs. For example, women, particularly survivors of sexual violence, require access to sexual and reproductive health services. Women and girls' vulnerabilities are often exacerbated in crisis contexts.

While participating in activities such as food distribution, firewood collection, and travel to and from latrines and water points, for example, they may be separated from protective family structures and face increased risks of trafficking, SGBV, including sexual exploitation and abuse, or other harm. Rape in conflict situations can increase the incidence of HIV/AIDS, affecting not only women but also their families. Conflict also increases the incidence of disability, and women with disabilities can face particular risks including social stigma and isolation, difficulty accessing humanitarian assistance, unmet health care needs, and higher rates of SGBV and other forms of violence during and after conflict.

Finally, women and girls act as combatants and in other capacities associated with armed forces, but demobilization, disarmament, and reintegration (DDR) programs often fail to take into account their distinct needs. Women ex-combatants are often grouped with those who have been kept as 'wives', despite distinct experiences and recovery needs. Women who have played a leadership role in a military structure are often reluctant to return to the roles that are expected of them when conflict ends, and women and girls associated with armed forces in any capacity require appropriate support to recover from physical and psychological trauma and rebuild their lives successfully.

For all of these reasons, it is vital that relief, recovery and rebuilding efforts meet the distinct needs of women and children in crises, while preventing sexual exploitation and abuse by those meant to help. Critical protection activities including prevention and response to SGBV should be prioritized in emergencies alongside other life-saving assistance. Women and girls must be able to access all humanitarian assistance programs safely and equitably, from water and sanitation to food aid and shelter, along with education, reproductive health care, and livelihood activities. This work begins by ensuring women's participation in the design of relief and recovery projects, which helps secure the explicit and systematic integration of gender and protection issues into response efforts. And women must have the opportunity to shape agendas and inform priorities for transitional justice and accountability, for the reconstruction of infrastructure and restoration of basic services, and for rebuilding economies in ways that offer opportunity for themselves and their families.

Supporting Women's Equal Access to Relief and Recovery Assistance

The United States is working with its partners to develop and implement relief and recovery assistance programs that address the needs of women and girls, mitigate risks to their safety, and reflect their perspectives and priorities. We do this through dedicated State and USAID programs focused on prevention and response to SGBV, provision of reproductive health care, and broader efforts to ensure all relief and recovery programming is accessible to women and girls. We have supported the development of a toolkit on reproductive health in emergencies, and training modules for NGOs on the prevention of sexual exploitation and abuse (SEA) of beneficiaries. We are also looking at ways to minimize risk to women and girls in humanitarian crises through supporting new technologies, such as a program to provide fuel efficient cookstoves to women in and around the Dadaab refugee camp in Kenya. This is part of a broader effort to familiarize the humanitarian community with best practices in fuel and firewood interventions, so that women and girls do not have to risk their safety when gathering firewood. We are also supporting access to education in emergencies for displaced children and youth. For example, in the Darfuri refugee camps in Chad, we are ensuring that secondary education programs are accessible to both girls and boys.

Investments in women's economic empowerment can also support crisis recovery and stability by empowering women and girls as agents of positive change and early recovery. For example, we fund literacy and livelihood programs in Pakistan, Afghanistan and the DRC to improve women's prospects when they return to their countries or communities of origin after displacement. And in Cote d'Ivoire, we support cash-for-work opportunities for women to engage in community clean-up activities to help them and their households recover from displacement and conflict.

Developing the National Action Plan

In instituting this National Action Plan, the United States joins countries around the world in accelerating the implementation of United Nations Security Council Resolution 1325 (2000), the first resolution adopted by the Security Council to recognize the crucial role of women in restoring and maintaining peace and security. Resolution 1325 and its subsequent, related resolutions—1820 (2008), 1888 (2009), 1889 (2009), and 1960 (2010)—aim, *inter alia*, to increase women's participation in all efforts related to peace and security and to strengthen the protection of women in situations of armed conflict. The United States drafted and presented three of these resolutions, including Resolution 1888, which established the position of the Special Representative of the Secretary General on Sexual Violence in Conflict, and remains a strong supporter of international and multilateral efforts to support the Women, Peace, and Security agenda. This plan expands on efforts at the Security Council by addressing the agenda's core pillars, to include taking action in a broad array of situations which do not necessarily fall within the scope of that body's mandate.

This Plan represents a government-wide effort to leverage U.S. diplomatic, defense, and development resources to improve the participation of women in peace and conflict prevention processes, protect women and girls from SGBV, and help ensure that women have full and equal access to relief and recovery resources. To ensure a whole of government perspective in developing the Plan, over the course of a year the White House National Security Staff assembled representatives from the Departments of State, Defense (DoD), Justice, Treasury, and Homeland Security (DHS), and the U.S. Mission to the UN (USUN), the U.S. Agency for International Development (USAID), the U.S. Centers for Disease Control and Prevention (CDC), and the Office of the U.S Trade Representative (USTR) to initiate and coordinate commitments.

These agencies each created internal working groups to provide input into the National Action Plan. Agency working groups consulted with staff in Washington and collected information from both diplomatic and development missions at U.S. Embassies, as well as at DoD's Unified Combatant Commands. Importantly, U.S. representatives in the field engaged in consultations with women and women's organizations, gender equality advocates, and government interlocutors to ensure that their perspectives and interests informed the Plan. Additionally, the interagency group conducted consultations with representatives of civil society in the United States and congressional staff to inform this document.

Based on these consultations, we have identified several priorities for advancing women's equality and empowerment in peace and security. We are confident that the actions proposed in this document are high-impact, necessary, achievable, and informed by those charged with implementation on the ground.

National Objectives and Action Framework

A directed by the Executive Order, the U.S. National Action Plan is targeted at meeting the following five high-level objectives:

- **National Integration and Institutionalization:** Through interagency coordination, policy development, enhanced professional training and education, and evaluation, the United States Government will institutionalize a gender-responsive approach to its diplomatic, development, and defense-related work in conflict-affected environments.

- **Participation in Peace Processes and Decision-making:** The United States Government will improve the prospects for inclusive, just, and sustainable peace by promoting and strengthening women's rights and effective leadership and substantive participation in peace processes, conflict prevention, peacebuilding, transitional processes, and decision-making institutions in conflict-affected environments.

- **Protection from Violence:** The United States Government will strengthen its efforts to prevent—and protect women and children from—harm, exploitation, discrimination, and abuse, including sexual and gender-based violence and trafficking in persons, and to hold perpetrators accountable in conflict-affected environments.

- **Conflict Prevention:** The United States Government will promote women's roles in conflict prevention, improve conflict early-warning and response systems through the integration of gender perspectives, and invest in women and girls' health, education, and economic opportunity to create conditions for stable societies and lasting peace.

- **Access to Relief and Recovery:** The United States Government will respond to the distinct needs of women and children in conflict-affected disasters and crises, including by providing safe, equitable access to humanitarian assistance.

To guide our efforts, the Action Framework below details the outcomes we seek, as well as the coordinated, exemplary actions agencies plan to pursue in order to achieve our objectives, recognizing that agencies may implement additional actions as appropriate.

1. National Integration and Institutionalization

Through interagency coordination, policy development, enhanced professional training and education, and evaluation, the United States Government will institutionalize a gender-sensitive approach to its diplomatic, development, and defense-related work in conflict-affected environments.

Outcome 1.1: Agencies establish and improve policy frameworks to support achievements in gender equality and women's empowerment throughout our diplomacy, development, and defense work.	Actions	Implementing Department or Agency
	Incorporate NAP objectives in strategic and operational planning, such as Bureau and Mission Strategic and Resource Plans (BSRPs and MSRPs) and Operational Plans, as appropriate. Disseminate guidance to all operating units on gender integration.	State, USAID
	Establish comprehensive, revised Agency-level policy on gender integration and women's empowerment by the end of 2011 through existing Gender Policy Task Team.	USAID
	Incorporate NAP objectives into appropriate DoD strategic guidance and planning documents.	DoD

	Actions	Implementing Department or Agency
Outcome 1.2: **Agencies enhance staff capacity for applying a gender-sensitive approach to diplomacy, development, and defense in conflict-affected environments.**	Ensure all relevant U.S. personnel and contractors receive appropriate training on Women, Peace, and Security issues, including instruction on the value of inclusive participation in conflict prevention, peace processes, and security initiatives, international human rights law and international humanitarian law, protection of civilians, prevention of SGBV, prevention of sexual exploitation and abuse (SEA), and combating trafficking in persons (TIP). Training mechanisms may include: Pre-deployment and in-theater training for members of the U.S. military and civilians, as well as Professional Military Education, including Commanders' courses, and intermediate and senior service schools. Introductory gender and C-TIP training for all USAID Foreign Service and Civil Service Officers, Personal Service Contractors, and Foreign Service Nationals and specialized training in gender analysis to personnel posting to conflict-affected countries or working on conflict issues. Training for State foreign service and civil service personnel, including senior management, and envoys and mediation team members. Training for CDC personnel working in conflict-affected countries to mainstream gender considerations into the design, implementation, and monitoring and evaluation of CDC research and programs.	State, USAID, DoD, CDC
	Provide technical assistance to decision-makers in headquarters and in the field on how to develop gender-sensitive programs.	State, USAID, CDC

	Actions	Implementing Department or Agency
Outcome 1.3: **Agencies establish mechanisms to promote accountability for implementation of their respective gender-related policies in conflict-affected environments.**	Designate one or more officers, as appropriate, as responsible for coordination of implementation of the NAP.	State, DoD, USAID
	Establish an annual award to honor individuals or operating units performing exceptional and innovative work to address gender equality and female empowerment in conflict-affected environments, and to promote the principles embodied in UNSCR 1325.	State, USAID, USUN
	Incorporate an assessment of gender integration into after action reviews (for USAID, those after action reviews pertaining to crisis response), and establish processes for addressing cases where gender issues are not being adequately considered in crisis response and conflict prevention environments.	State, USAID, CDC

	Actions	Implementing Department or Agency
Outcome 1.4: **Agencies establish processes to evaluate and learn from activities undertaken in support of WPS initiatives.**	Utilize innovations in foreign assistance coordination and tracking systems where appropriate, including gender cross-cutting indicators, sector-specific gender-sensitive indicators, and revised gender key issue definitions to support budgeting, operational planning, and performance management related to the NAP.	State, USAID, CDC
	Develop and improve data collection mechanisms to track and report progress on WPS objectives, assess lessons learned, and identify best practices from existing programs.	DoD, USUN
	Identify and share with U.S. Government agencies lessons learned and best practices from multilateral development banks' experiences in post conflict and transitioning countries.	Treasury

2. Participation in Peace Processes and Decision-making

The United States Government will improve the prospects for inclusive, just, and sustainable peace by promoting and strengthening women's rights and effective leadership and substantive participation in peace processes, conflict prevention, peacebuilding, transitional processes, and decision-making institutions in conflict-affected environments.

Rwandan women voting by secret ballot in district-level elections. In 2008, Rwanda became the first nation with women making up more than half of parliament—they secured 56.25% of seats.
Photo Credit: Institute for Inclusive Security

DUE TO COPYRIGHT RESTRICTIONS SOME OR ALL IMAGES ARE NOT INCLUDED

	Actions	Implementing Department or Agency
Outcome 2.1: **More women are effectively engaged in peace negotiations, security initiatives, conflict prevention, peace-building-including formal and informal processes--and decision-making during all phases of conflict prevention and resolution, and transition.**	U.S. Government delegations serve as a model for the inclusion of women in talks and negotiations concerning conflict resolution, peacebuilding, and/or political transitions; and advocate for the integration of women and gender perspectives in processes in which the U.S. is involved.	State, USAID, USUN
	Advocate for the inclusion of women in senior UN positions.	State, USUN
	Support the participation and leadership roles of women from all backgrounds, including minorities and women with disabilities, in peace negotiations, donor conferences, security sector reform efforts, transitional justice and accountability processes, and other related decision-making forums including those led by the UN and other international and regional organizations, and including capacity building for such actors as female candidates, female members of government, women in the security sector, and women in civil society.	State, USAID, USUN

	Actions	Implementing Department or Agency
Outcome 2.1: *Continued* **More women are effectively engaged in peace negotiations, security initiatives, conflict prevention, peace-building--including formal and informal processes--and decision-making during all phases of conflict prevention and resolution, and transition.**	Assist partner governments in improving the recruitment and retention of women, including minorities and other historically marginalized women, into government ministries and the incorporation of women's perspectives into peace and security policy.	State, USAID, DoD
	Provide assistance to support women's political participation and leadership in fragile environments and during democratic transitions, including capacity building for such actors as female candidates, female members of government, women in the security sector, and women in civil society.	State, USAID, USUN
	Provide common guidelines and training to assist partner nations to integrate women and their perspectives into their security sectors.	State, DoD, USUN
	Provide support for NGOs to track, analyze, and advocate on behalf of the engagement of women and women's organizations in peace processes.	State, USAID
	Expand emphasis on gender analysis and support to local organizations, including women's peacebuilding organizations, in conflict mitigation and reconciliation programming.	State, USAID, USUN
	Leverage the participation of female U.S. military personnel to encourage and model gender integration and reach out to female and male populations in partner nations.	State, DoD
	Increase partner nation women's participation in U.S. funded training programs for foreign police, judicial, and military personnel, including professional military education (PME), as well as exchange programs, conferences, and seminars.	State, DoD
	Mobilize men as allies in support of women's leadership and participation in security-related processes and decision-making.	State, USAID, USUN
Outcome 2.2: **Laws, policies, and practices in partner states promote and strengthen gender equality at national and local levels.**	**Actions**	**Implementing Department or Agency**
	Through high level diplomacy and technical assistance, encourage nations to develop laws that promote and protect women's rights, including through the criminalization of violence against women and girls and adoption of effective procedural laws, as well as through laws and policies that advance women's participation in parliaments, the judicial sector, and other political, peace, and/or security decision-making bodies, including those calling for affirmative measures, where appropriate.	State, USAID, Justice

	Actions	Implementing Department or Agency
Outcome 2.2: *Continued* **Laws, policies, and practices in partner states promote and strengthen gender equality at national and local levels.**	Provide diplomatic, development, and technical assistance to build the capacity of legislative, judicial, and law enforcement actors to develop, implement, and enforce laws that promote and protect women's rights; and civil society to advocate for the development and implementation of such laws.	State, USAID, Justice
	Assist partner nations in building the capacity of their Defense Ministries to develop, implement, and enforce policies and military justice systems that promote and protect women's rights.	DoD

3. Protection from Violence

The United States Government will strengthen its efforts to prevent—and protect women and children from—harm, exploitation, discrimination, and abuse, including sexual and gender-based violence and trafficking in persons, and to hold perpetrators accountable in conflict- affected environments.

	Actions	Implementing Agency or Department
Outcome 3.1: **Risks of SGBV in crisis and conflict-affected environments are decreased through the increased capacity of individuals, communities, and protection actors to address the threats and vulnerability associated with SGBV.**	Work to improve the capacity of the UN system and key protection and humanitarian actors, including members of the Humanitarian Cluster system, to prevent and respond to SGBV in conflict affected and crisis settings, to include development and implementation of training, guidance, and other operational tools; and promote better coordination and sharing of information across UN country teams in order to develop and implement holistic strategies on SGBV.	State, USAID, CDC, USUN
	Advocate for UN peacekeeping missions to have strong mandates on protection of civilians (POC), including on sexual and gender-based violence (SGBV), and provide diplomatic support for initiatives in the UN General Assembly Special Committee on Peacekeeping Operations (C-34) and budget committees to build the capacity and provide operational tools for POC and prevention of SGBV.	State, USUN
	Incorporate modules on protection, rights, and specific needs of women in conflict into training provided to partner militaries and security personnel.	DoD
	Require USG humanitarian assistance implementing partners to have Codes of Conduct consistent with the Inter-Agency Standing Committee's (IASC) core principles on protection of beneficiaries from sexual exploitation and abuse, and monitor and promote partner compliance.	State, USAID
	Support education and awareness initiatives for U.S. Government civilian contractors and aid workers on the prevention of sexual exploitation and abuse in crisis and conflict-affected environments.	State, USAID, DoD

	Actions	Implementing Agency or Department
Outcome 3.1: *Continued* **Risks of SGBV in crisis and conflict-affected environments are decreased through the increased capacity of individuals, communities, and protection actors to address the threats and vulnerability associated with SGBV.**	Support research, programming and learning on the use of technology with the potential to improve the safety of women and girls in conflict settings (e.g. solar lighting, solar or methane-conversion cook stoves, provision of cell phones as part of an early warning system, and mobile justice mechanisms), consistent with available best practices and international guidelines.	State, USAID, USUN
	Provide support for a range of appropriate services and tools to assist and empower vulnerable women and girls, including medical services, psychosocial services, and legal services, as well as opportunities for livelihood training, education, and rest and recreation (e.g. athletics, art, and play); promote equitable access to these services for women and girls with disabilities	State, USAID
	Issue updated public guidance for U.S. Government partners on addressing SGBV in humanitarian assistance programming, including proposal guidance for SGBV prevention and response programming in disaster situations.	USAID
	Collaborate with U.S. personnel abroad, embassy staff, and non-governmental and governmental international partners, as appropriate, to combat exploitation and violence against women and girls by sharing training resources, public awareness tools, and victim referral assistance.	DHS
	Develop an evidence base for context-specific risk factors for SGBV using robust, scientific, qualitative and quantitative methods; and translate research findings into programs and policies.	CDC
	Evaluate the impact of programs and policies to prevent and respond to SGBV to ensure that available resources are being implemented as efficiently and effectively as possible.	CDC

Strengthening Women's Participation in Security Forces and Peacekeeping Operations

The United States seeks to increase women's participation in security forces in order to prevent conflict and build peace in areas affected by war, violence, and insecurity. For example, as part of its global peacekeeping capacity building mission, the Department of State funds, and both State and DOD implement the Global Peace Operations Initiative (GPOI), which has facilitated the training of 2,451 female peacekeepers worldwide—84 percent of whom are from African countries. This initiative has focused on Women, Peace and Security education activities by supporting instruction on prevention of sexual exploitation and abuse (SEA), prevention of SGBV, and human rights training in its 59 partner countries and in most of the 43 GPOI peace support operations training centers around the world. Beginning in 2011, GPOI has supported the pre-deployment training of Peruvian women peacekeepers focused on Women, Peace, and Security issues in support of the United Nations Stabilization Mission in Haiti (MINUSTAH).

In Afghanistan, the Department of Defense is working to increase women's participation in the security sector. U.S. service men and women work side by side to model the successful integration of women into the armed forces, and U.S. and Afghan officers provide instruction, mentoring, and support to female soldiers in the Afghan National Army. In addition, through the Ministry of Defense Advisor's (MoDA) Program, Department of Defense civilian personnel are working with Afghanistan's Ministry of Defense and Ministry of the Interior to increase the number of women in the Afghan National Army and Police. The first class of female Afghan soldiers graduated from the Afghan National Army's Female Officer Candidate School in September 2010. In 2012, 10 percent of the Afghan military academy's class will be women, and by 2014 Afghanistan expects to field 5,000 women Afghan National Police officers.

	Actions	Implementing Agency or Department
Outcome 3.2: **Laws, policies, and reconciliation, transitional justice, and accountability mechanisms designed to combat exploitation, abuse, discrimination, and violence against women and girls are developed and implemented at national and locals.**	Support the development of effective accountability and transitional justice mechanisms that address crimes committed against women and girls and reduce impunity.	State, USAID, DoD, Justice
	Support through diplomatic efforts and development and technical assistance the creation of effective measures to investigate SGBV promptly, effectively, independently, and impartially; and to bring those responsible for SGBV to justice. Support the establishment of mechanisms for survivors and witnesses of SGBV so that they can make complaints safely and confidentially, and build capacity so that there can be appropriate follow-up to these complaints. Where appropriate, support compensation or reparations for survivors and their families.	State, USAID, Justice
	Use public diplomacy and outreach capabilities to help ensure that survivors of SGBV understand the accountability options available to them and to disseminate the message that perpetrators of SGBV are held accountable and that impunity will not be tolerated.	State
	Assist multilateral and international organizations in developing appropriate mechanisms for sexual assault prevention, response, and accountability, and combating sexual exploitation and abuse (SEA) among their own personnel. Establish standard operating procedures for USG to follow up on cases of SEA by international personnel to ensure accountability.	State, DoD, USAID
	Collaborate with foreign law enforcement counterparts, as appropriate, in joint efforts to disrupt and dismantle transnational criminal organizations engaged in human smuggling and trafficking, including but not limited to forced child labor, and engaged in other forms of exploitation and abuse of women and children.	DHS, Justice
	Actions	**Implementing Agency or Department**
Outcome 3.3: **Interventions are improved to prevent trafficking in persons and protect trafficking survivors in conflict and crisis-affected areas.**	Engage with international and/or civil society organizations to ensure that standard operating procedures are in place to prevent human trafficking, especially among refugees and internally displaced persons (IDPs), including appropriate assistance and procedures for unaccompanied minors, to identify potential trafficked persons, and to refer survivors to appropriate service providers. As appropriate, provide support to international and civil society organizations to set up emergency care services for trafficking survivors.	State, Justice
	Advocate for the inclusion of language in UN peacekeeping operations mandates directing a responsibility to report on trafficking, as appropriate.	State, USUN

	Actions	Implementing Agency or Department
Outcome 3.3: *Continued* **Interventions are improved to prevent trafficking in persons and protect trafficking survivors in conflict and crisis-affected areas.**	Engage with international and/or civil society organizations to ensure that standard operating procedures are in place to prevent human trafficking, especially among refugees and internally displaced persons (IDPs), including appropriate assistance and procedures for unaccompanied minors, to identify potential trafficked persons, and to refer survivors to appropriate service providers. As appropriate, provide support to international and civil society organizations to set up emergency care services for trafficking survivors.	State, Justice
	Advocate for the inclusion of language in UN peacekeeping operations mandates directing a responsibility to report on trafficking, as appropriate.	State, USUN
	Promote establishment of local coalitions or taskforces comprised of relevant government authorities and civil society organizations to combat human trafficking as part of the justice reform measures in post-conflict areas.	State, USAID
	Implement the USAID Counter Trafficking Code of Conduct holding personnel, contractors, sub-contractors, and grantees to the highest ethical standards with regard to trafficking, and develop a new Trafficking in Persons Policy with a focus on increasing anti-trafficking initiatives in conflict-affected areas.	USAID
	Implement agency-wide training to educate staff on ethical standards related to the USAID Counter Trafficking Code of Conduct and provide technical assistance to personnel to design, implement, monitor and evaluate effective anti-trafficking interventions, including in conflict-affected areas.	USAID
	Maintain a zero tolerance policy with regard to trafficking in persons for U.S. military and civilian personnel.	DoD
	Advance collaborative efforts to prevent trafficking in persons by sharing training and public awareness resources with U.S. personnel abroad, embassy staff and other international partners, and by additionally sharing investigative resources with foreign law enforcement counterparts as appropriate.	DHS
	Coordinate implementation of the anti-trafficking-related items of the NAP with the ongoing work of the U.S. Presidential Interagency Task Force to Monitor and Combat Trafficking in Persons and the Senior Policy Operating Group on Trafficking in Persons.	State, DOD, Justice, DHS, USAID

	Actions	Implementing Agency or Department
Outcome 3.4: **Men and boys are themselves better protected from SGBV, and are mobilized as partners in the prevention of SGBV and other risks of harm, exploitation, and abuse in their communities.**	Provide support for advocacy campaigns and programs designed to reduce family and community level violence.	State, USAID
	Increase attention to the needs of male survivors in SGBV prevention and response programs.	State, USAID
	Develop programs that address harmful norms and practices contributing to SGBV and other forms of exploitation and abuse, through the engagement of a broad range of potential allies, including religious and tribal leaders, youth, the business community, and men and boys.	State, USAID

4. Conflict Prevention

The United States Government will promote women's roles in conflict prevention, improve conflict early-warning and response systems through the integration of gender perspectives, and invest in women and girls' health, education, and economic opportunity to create conditions for stable societies and lasting peace.

U.S. Marine Corps Cpl. Sarah B. Furrel teaches Afghan girls to count numbers at a school in Now Zad, Afghanistan.
Photo Credit: Cpl. Albert F. Hunt/U.S. Marine Corps

	Actions	Implementing Department or Agency
Outcome 4.1: **Conflict early warning and response systems include gender-specific data and are responsive to SGBV, and women participate in early warning, preparedness, and response initiatives.**	Integrate protocols and support opportunities to share best practices for gender analysis in conflict mapping and reporting, including for mass atrocity prevention and stabilization funding. Review conflict early warning systems and conflict assessment methodologies, including the Interagency Conflict Assessment Framework, to assess and strengthen the integration of gender in these tools.	State, USAID, DoD
	Ensure the inclusion of a broad range of perspectives from women and youth to inform policy, strategy and programming decisions.	State, USUN
	Share and utilize relevant data from the Women's Agriculture Empowerment Index and the Demographic and Health Survey in support of conflict prevention, early warning, and response activities.	USAID
	Actively engage women in planning and implementing disaster and emergency preparedness and risk reduction activities, including regarding how police can better interact with women in their role as first responders.	USAID, DoD
	Provide diplomatic and development support for community-based early warning and response activities, such as empowering local communities to develop strategies to prevent and respond to outbreaks or escalations of violence and conflict.	State, USAID, CDC
	Provide diplomatic and development support for women's coalitions working to mitigate conflict and related activity, helping to ensure active participation by minorities and other particularly marginalized women.	State, USAID
	Identify and share relevant multilateral development bank databases, such as the World Bank's Gender Stats, a one-stop source of information on gender at the country level, drawn from national statistics agencies, UN databases, World Bank surveys, and other sources.	Treasury

	Actions	Implementing Department or Agency
Outcome 4.2: **Women and girls participate in economic recovery, and have increased access to health care and education services.**	Provide diplomatic and development support to advance women's economic empowerment, including through cash for work programs, increased access to land, credit, and other enterprise support activities.	State, USAID
	Promote access to primary, secondary and vocational education for children and youth in countries affected by violence or conflict, with special incentives for the attendance and retention of girls, taking into account related special protection needs.	State, USAID
	Support women's and girls' increased access to health services, including reproductive and maternal health care.	State, USAID, CDC
	Advocate for the operationalization within the multilateral development banks of the relevant information from the 2011 and 2012 World Development Reports on the role women can play both in preventing conflict and in promoting stability in post-conflict situations.	Treasury
	Create and strengthen private sector activities and new market opportunities through U.S. trade and investment programs, such as preference programs and Trade and Investment Framework Agreements, to assist women entrepreneurs grow their businesses.	USTR

5. Access to Relief and Recovery

The United States Government will respond to the distinct needs of women and children in conflict-affected disasters and crises, including by providing safe, equitable access to humanitarian assistance.

A flood-affected family receives USAID relief commodities in Luzon Province, Philippines.
Photo credit: Ben Hemmingway/USAID

	Actions	Implementing Department or Agency
Outcome 5.1: **Gender and protection issues are explicitly and systematically integrated and evaluated as part of responses to crisis and disaster.**	Promote women's, men's, and children's equal access to aid distribution mechanisms and services, including establishing or strengthening protocols for the safe and equitable delivery of humanitarian assistance.	State, USAID
	Support capacity building for local and international NGOs and multilateral organizations involved in disaster and crisis response to address the specific protection needs of women and girls, including preventing and responding to SGBV.	State, USAID, CDC

	Actions	Implementing Department or Agency
Outcome 5.1: *Continued* **Gender and protection issues are explicitly and systematically integrated and evaluated as part of responses to crisis and disaster.**	Support access to reproductive health in emergencies and humanitarian settings.	State, USAID, CDC
	Promote access to education in emergencies consistent with international guidelines and best practices.	State, USAID
	Support measures for the social and economic empowerment of women as part of crisis and disaster response, including support for livelihood activities.	State, USAID
	Ensure that U.S. Government crisis response and recovery teams have access to appropriate gender expertise, such as a designated gender advisor, to integrate gender considerations in U.S. Government-supported relief and recovery efforts.	State, USAID
	Ensure that USAID Disaster Assistance Response Team (DART) members deployed to crisis situations have been trained on the protection of women and girls in humanitarian operations.	USAID
	Advocate that multilateral development banks' post-conflict assessments, country assistance strategies, and operational programs in countries prone to or emerging from conflict reflect sound gender analysis and address the specific needs of women and girls.	Treasury

	Actions	Implementing Department or Agency
Outcome 5.2: **Relief and recovery assistance includes enhanced measures to prevent and respond to SGBV in conflict and post-conflict environments.**	Provide support for survivors of conflict, torture, and sexual violence, to include persons with disabilities, their families, and communities, through direct services, including trauma-informed services and sexual and reproductive healthcare.	State, USAID, CDC
	Encourage international organization and NGO partners to provide gender and SGBV training to staff members on existing international guidelines, such as the IASC Guidelines on GBV in Humanitarian Settings, the Sphere Project, and Standards Recommended by the IASC Task Force on Protection from Sexual Exploitation and Abuse (PSEA) in Humanitarian Crises.	State, USAID, CDC
	Make available to the public information and analysis on U.S. Government-supported gender-based violence programming in disaster contexts, post-conflict situations, and political transitions in order to promote learning and dissemination of best practices.	USAID
	Provide humanitarian protection through the administration of immigration benefits programs and other immigration mechanisms, as appropriate, to eligible individuals, including women and girls, in need of relief from persecution or urgent circumstances.	DHS

	Actions	Implementing Department or Agency
Outcome 5.3: **Reintegration and early recovery programs address the distinct needs of men and women.**	Support return and reintegration programs for refugees and internally displaced persons (IDPs) that address the needs of female returnees.	State, USAID
	Support demobilization, disarmament, and reintegration (DDR) programs, including sustainable livelihood alternatives, that address the distinct needs of male and female ex-combatants and those associated with armed forces in other capacities.	State, DoD, USUN, USAID

Coordination, Implementation, Monitoring, and Reporting

The goals set forth in this National Action Plan are the beginning, rather than the end, of effecting real and meaningful change. As directed by the Executive Order, within 150 days, State, DoD, and USAID will designate one or more officer or officers, as appropriate, as responsible for coordination and implementation, and will supplement this Plan by submitting to the Assistant to the President and National Security Advisor agency-specific Women, Peace, and Security implementation plans. These implementation plans will establish a full range of time-bound, measurable, and resourced actions State, DoD, and USAID will take to realize their commitments, and will include meaningful strategies for monitoring implementation and evaluating results.

To ensure all agencies involved in this effort act in close coordination as they work to implement the National Action Plan and, where appropriate, develop and execute their own agency-specific plans, the White House National Security Staff (NSS) will establish and chair an Interagency Policy Committee dedicated to Women, Peace, and Security (WPS IPC). The WPS IPC will monitor and review actions taken in support of U.S. national objectives, and will integrate the Women, Peace, and Security agenda in relevant national-level policies and strategies. For additional agencies with actions listed under this Plan, as well as for those agencies that may participate in future interagency discussions on Women, Peace, and Security, the WPS IPC will establish a mechanism to report progress. For countries of particular concern or countries that represent a unique opportunity, the IPC may coordinate government-wide country plans or provide a coordination function as individual agencies elect to develop country-level plans. The WPS IPC will also establish a mechanism for regular consultation with civil society representatives on the status of the National Action Plan's implementation. Participating agencies with a field presence will be encouraged to establish or maintain similar mechanisms to promote regular consultation with women and civil society organizations in relevant countries and regions.

Working through the WPS IPC, agencies will report annually to the National Security Council Deputies Committee on progress made toward achieving the commitments contained in the National Action Plan and agency-level implementation plans, which the Assistant to the President and National Security Advisor shall draw upon to provide an annual report to the President. Progress in implementing the objectives of the National Action Plan will be monitored and evaluated against specific indicators, to be identified at the direction of the WPS IPC.

This work will build upon ongoing initiatives across the U.S. Government to ensure transparency, accountability, and effectiveness in our investments in diplomacy, development, and defense. We will analyze the success of our own staff training, enhance our efforts to collect sex-disaggregated data in conflict-affected areas, and establish metrics to identify where women's participation is increasing and their protection is enhanced. All of these efforts will be informed by the work of multilateral partners, including UN agencies, and other countries, as we work to develop rigorous monitoring and evaluation tools to advance the Women, Peace, and Security agenda. The Administration looks forward to working with Congress to ensure support for initiatives under this Plan.

Finally, in 2015, the National Security Staff will coordinate a comprehensive review of, and update to, this National Action Plan, which will be informed, in part, by consultation with international partners and relevant civil society organizations.

Partnerships and Collaboration

The goals set forward in this Plan can only be realized through partnership and collaboration with other governments, international organizations, and civil society actors, as well as innovative partnership with the private sector. Central among these partners are the women and organizations throughout the world working every day to build sustainable peace and security and to champion women as vital, equal partners. Together, we can coordinate and leverage resources, learn from the successes and challenges of others, and design and implement inclusive assistance programs that build local capacity and promote sustainable outcomes.

Through our bilateral diplomacy, development assistance, and security cooperation in countries affected by crisis and conflict, we will support existing national government efforts to protect and empower women as agents of peace and security, and advocate for greater inclusion and efforts in cases where the voices of women need to be amplified and supported.

Promoting Women's Leadership in Countries in Transition

Today, millions of people living in the Middle East and North Africa are facing unprecedented opportunities to build more inclusive, democratic societies. The Department of State and USAID are working to ensure that women will be full partners in these journeys.

For example, in advance of Tunisia's elections in October 2011, the United States helped local organizations train candidates, including women, educate voters and enhance voter participation, and raise public awareness of equal rights for all, including women and minorities, through mass media. In Egypt, we are working to enhance women's political, economic, and social status through capacity building for women political leaders, scholarships for girls, and microfinance initiatives in rural areas. In Libya, we are engaging with our international and Libyan partners to ensure that women play an equal role in rebuilding their country's government and civil society institutions.

In Iraq, the U.S. will continue partnering with the people of Iraq to bring women to the forefront of efforts to advance peace and security, promote economic growth, and ensure democratic governance. We will target more than $17.3 million to advance women's civil, political, economic, cultural, and social rights through efforts such as the Iraqi Women's Democracy Initiative. Successful transitions to stable and prosperous democracies in the Middle East will hinge on strong protections for women's rights and the inclusion of women's voices. The U.S. is committed to working with the women of the region to ensure the successful transformation of their countries into vital and vibrant democracies.

We will partner with other countries, both donors and those with specific experience dealing with the challenges of conflict, to amplify our bilateral assistance and advocacy efforts and ensure their efficient coordination. These partnerships will reflect the sound principles set forth in the Paris Declaration on Aid Effectiveness, the Accra Agenda for Action, and the Busan Partnership for Effective Development Cooperation, which underscore the importance of country ownership, donor coordination, inclusive partnerships, harmonization, alignment, results, and mutual accountability.

Through our multilateral engagement, we will endeavor to ensure that the work of the United Nations and other international, regional, and sub-regional organizations upholds the principle that women must have an equal voice in addressing challenges to peace and security. When these institutions are themselves engaged as actors in conflict- and post-conflict situations, we will, as appropriate, assist and cooperate with them to help ensure that development, humanitarian assistance, and peace and security operations integrate a strong gender perspective and effectively serve the interests of women and girls. And we will continue to support the efforts of UN Women on this front.

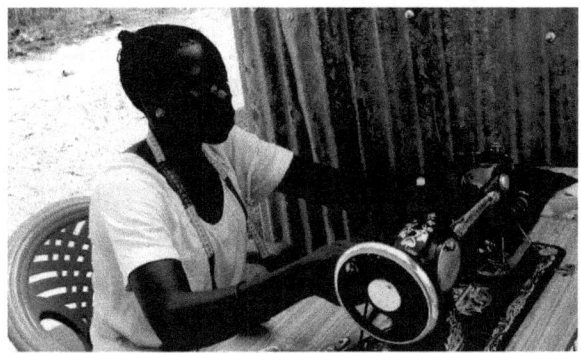

A young woman works on a skirt as part of a USAID-funded project south of Juba, Republic of South Sudan.
Photo credit: Laura Meissner/USAID

In all our efforts, we will seek collaborative partnerships with non-governmental organizations active at the national, regional, and international levels, as well as the private sector. We will work with academic and other research institutions and practitioners to understand and expand the information available on the role of women in all aspects of peace and security, so that policy-makers across the government can reach more informed decisions on issues of peace and security, how best to invest our resources, and where to direct our efforts.

Finally we expect civil society, which informed the development of this Plan, to hold us accountable to these commitments, to help us learn from activities and approaches implemented under the Plan, and to contribute to future revisions of the Plan.

Call to Action

War is a regular and recurring feature of the human experience. In many instances, conflicts have recurred or been prolonged in significant part because women—those who suffered the worst of the violence and bore the burden of reconstruction—were excluded from the negotiating table and the benefits of peace.

DUE TO COPYRIGHT RESTRICTIONS
SOME OR ALL IMAGES ARE NOT INCLUDED

Today, at the beginning of the 21ˢᵗ century, we must take the simple and long overdue steps necessary to help stop cycles of armed conflict. Women can and must ensure

To celebrate the 10th anniversary of UN Security Council Resolution 1325 on Women, Peace, and Security, the UN organized dialogues in 25 post-conflict countries between womenís peacebuilding organizations, women community leaders, and senior UN leadership. *Photo credit: Institute for Inclusive Security*

their voices, experiences, and needs play an equal role in promoting peace and security efforts around the world. We can help them do this by strengthening protections for women from violence during and after war; and ensuring their participation in peace negotiations and relief and recovery efforts. And we must take proactive efforts to build women's capacities to prevent war and promote stability—by providing girls and women access to tools such as education, economic opportunity, and health care.

The United States is committed to ensuring that this National Action Plan on Women, Peace, and Security does not begin and end merely as words on paper. Today we dedicate ourselves to bringing the ideas and goals expressed in this document to life in our work around the world, and commit the United States to the essential effort of empowerment and sustained, equitable peace for all.

www.ingramcontent.com/pod-product-compliance
Lightning Source LLC
Chambersburg PA
CBHW052028280526
45793CB00005B/1164